Mr. McCloskey's Marvelous Mallards

The Making of
MAKE WAY FOR DUCKLINGS

Emma Bland Smith   Illustrated by **Becca Stadtlander**

CALKINS CREEK

AN IMPRINT OF ASTRA BOOKS FOR YOUNG READERS

New York

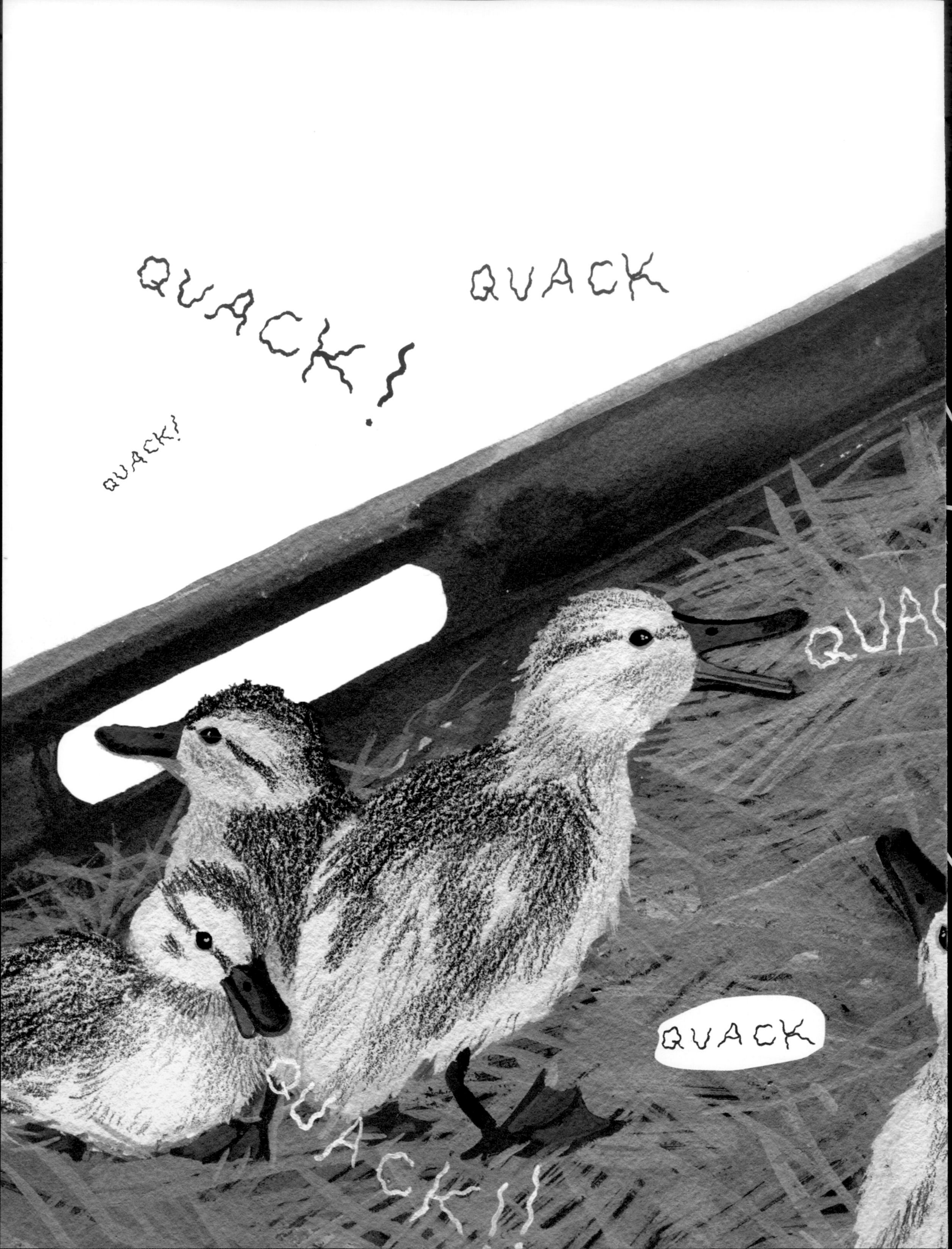
QUACK!
QUACK
QUACK!
QUACK
QUACK!!

You can't draw ducks
unless you live with them.
—Robert McCloskey

Robert McCloskey stood back and studied his sketches. He shook his head. *These ducks are not right*, he thought. That wasn't how a duck waddled, or fell on her behind, or flapped his wings. He paced around his New York City studio.

How did he get himself into this duck-drawing mess anyway?

It had all started four years before, when he was
in art school in Boston. Walking to and from classes,
he'd laughed at the funny mallard ducks in the
park. He fed them peanuts and watched as they
splashed and dove in the lake. Once he ran into
a whole family on the sidewalk waddling into the
Public Garden in a long orderly row.

Mr. McCloskey finished art school and ended up in New York City. A few years later, he returned to Boston for a visit. He'd completed his first children's book and was wondering what to write about next. Again, he saw those funny mallards. He remembered the family of ducks he'd seen on the sidewalk.

He smiled. His eyes sparkled.

And there it was—his story! A pair of mallard ducks, looking for a safe place to raise their ducklings in a busy city. Bingo!

It had taken him quite a while to get the words on paper. Then, when he finally had a rough story, it was time to draw the illustrations to go with the words.

And that's how he found himself, today, scratching his head, searching his memory, picturing those ducks, trying his darndest to draw them.

It was, let's just say, harder than he'd expected.

He brought the sketches to his editor. She was not impressed. He didn't blame her.

I can do better, he thought. *I* have *to do better!*

I need to see actual *ducks,* he decided, and went uptown to the science museum.

For days, Mr. McCloskey studied the stuffed ducks at the museum. He looked at them from the right, and from the left. He gathered more scientific information about ducks than he knew what to do with. He sketched and erased and started from scratch.

But when he stood back and looked at the sketches, he frowned. These ducks were just okay. And "just okay" wasn't good enough. His editor would never accept these drawings!

I can do better, he thought. *I have to do better!*
What else would help? Live models! That was it!

He came home with a box full of tiny ducklings—
very alive (and very LOUD)!

For the next few months, the ducklings lived in
Mr. McCloskey's studio. It wasn't easy using them as
models—they did not cooperate! They wouldn't stay
still, and they clumped together instead of walking
in a row.

What's more, they made a terrible mess, and they
woke everyone at dawn with their infernal quacking!
(Mr. McCloskey's roommate was not amused.)

QUACK!

But Mr. McCloskey was determined. He crawled around studying the ducklings. He sketched them waddling and running, plopping down and jumping up. He crawled around after them so much, his knees just about gave out on him!

His sketches were getting there. But they still weren't good enough—not for his editor, and not for him. Even the ducks didn't seem to think much of them.

I can do better, he thought. *I have to do better!*

He was willing to do whatever it took to make these drawings perfect. So he thought a bit and then—he did what any reasonable person would do: He went out and bought *more* ducks! Grown ones, this time.

He focused his mind. It was time to tackle the
hardest illustrations of all: flying. How on earth
was he going to draw an airborne mallard?

The weeks passed by. Mr McCloskey drew and drew and drew. He worked on the writing too, cutting words and letting the drawings tell the action. He was almost there.

And time was almost up because the ducks had become simply impossible!

They hogged the bathtub, splashed something awful, and caused leaks in the ceiling underneath.

It wasn't really their fault—being cooped up in a studio was no life for a duck. They needed to go.

So Mr. McCloskey drove the ducks out to a friend's place in the country. There, they could make all the mess they wanted and quack as early as they liked! It was just the right place for a flock of noisy ducks.

QUACK!!

He said goodbye. They quacked back at him.

In his studio again, he went over the manuscript, holding his breath.

He turned the last page . . .

. . . and grinned.

The drawings were better than just okay.

They were better than getting there.

They were absolutely top-notch!

The work hadn't been easy. It hadn't always been fun, either. But it was the greatest thing he'd ever done. (He felt sure the ducks would have approved too.)

And although he was normally a calm sort of fellow, Mr. McCloskey grabbed his drawings and practically flew uptown to show them to his editor.

And this time . . .

. . . she was extremely impressed.

But what about children? They were the toughest judges of all, and the ones who really mattered.

When the book came out, *Make Way for Ducklings* was a hit!

All it took was six years, buckets of patience, a good supply of erasers, and a studio full of spirited ducks.

A Word from Jane McCloskey

I am grateful to Emma for bringing my father to life in this book.

Like the mallards, our family ended up on an island, and it was there that my father painted the illustrations for most of his books. In his studio, he did hundreds of sketches of my sister Sal and me, playing, crawling around, sitting, and doing art of our own.

Sal and I were both in *One Morning in Maine*, and in some crowd scenes in *Homer Price* and *Centerburg Tales*. (And Sal was in *Blueberries for Sal*, of course.)

We learned to sit still when he painted our portraits. I learned to keep still in a way that I never realized was unusual until a few years ago, when my dentist kept exclaiming at what a great patient I was!

I also learned patience and high standards from my father. From both him and my mother I learned to appreciate tolerance, decency, and, oh yeah, good food.

Neither my sister nor I, unfortunately, inherited my father's artistic abilities, though Sal's daughter, Samantha, carries that gene.

—*Jane McCloskey*, Maine

McCloskey's daughters, Sal and Jane, often modeled for their father and appear in several of his books. Jane credits him with teaching her patience and the ability to stay still for long periods of time!

Author's Note

Although *Make Way for Ducklings* is a story about mallard ducks, it is not known for sure whether the ducklings Robert McCloskey purchased as models were in fact mallards.

Make Way for Ducklings was Robert McCloskey's second book. Published when he was only twenty-seven years old, it won the prestigious Caldecott Award for illustration. (Four more of his picture books also garnered Caldecott acclaim.)

What made his work so special and unforgettable? McCloskey was a perfectionist, and believed in studying his subjects until he could portray them as accurately as possible, no matter how long it took. Another factor was his habit of taking inspiration from the real people and places around him.

Only when I was an adult did I make the connection that the girl in *Blueberries for Sal* was the very same little girl as the main character in *One Morning in Maine*. And I never thought about the two books the same way again.

Later, I learned that the people and settings in both books were directly inspired by Robert McCloskey's real life on an island in Maine—right down to daughters Sal and Jane, Mother with her blueberry pail, the two Mr. Condons, and Penny the English setter! I was enchanted. (Perhaps it's not a coincidence that four of my own books are set on islands!)

Writing and illustrating real life had been important to Mr. McCloskey since the beginning of his career. *Make Way for Ducklings* came out of his time in art school in Boston, when he would walk through the Public Garden and feed peanuts to the ducks. And *Lentil* and *Homer Price* were both plucked directly out of his childhood in small-town Ohio. No wonder these books feel so real and right.

More than seventy-five years after he began illustrating, Mr. McCloskey's books continue to touch readers on many levels. The common themes of home, family, and security were reassuring to children growing up in an era of escalating international tension. His works feel profoundly comforting and American—in the best sense of the word. (He has been compared to Norman Rockwell for the nostalgic, homey feelings his works provoke.) And yet, his clean lines have a modern sensibility that is refreshing and timeless.

Robert McCloskey's dedication, persistence, and insistence on research and accuracy combine with the charms of his characters and settings to create some of the most beloved books in children's literature.

About May Massee

It was his editor at Viking Press, May Massee, who put Robert McCloskey on his way to success in children's book writing. He visited her when he was only twenty, at the very end of art school, with a portfolio full of drawings of dragons, Greek heroes, and made-up landscapes. She told him, in so many words, to lighten up and draw what he knew—and to come back when he'd done so.

He spent the next several years in New York and Ohio, and when he visited Ms. Massee again, he brought her a draft of his first picture book, *Lentil*. She loved it.

Ms. Massee had an important role in the creation of *Make Way for Ducklings*, Mr. McCloskey's second book. She used her great experience and instinct to guide him in writing and editing the text, which changed enormously from start to finish.

She insisted that his books remain in the now-iconic single color (up until *Time of Wonder*, when Mr. McCloskey talked her into letting him expand into watercolor).

Ms. Massee edited the books of many other legendary children's book authors and illustrators, such as Marjorie Flack and Kurt Wiese (*The Story About Ping*), Munro Leaf and Robert Lawson (*The Story of Ferdinand*), and Ezra Jack Keats (*The Snowy Day*).

Today, there is a special exhibit and archive dedicated to her career, at Emporia State University in Kansas. For more information, visit emporia.edu/libraries-archives/special-collections-archives/access/special-collections/may-massee-collection.

McCloskey spent months sketching ducklings and ducks in his studio apartment in New York City's Greenwich Village. He shared the studio with friend Marc Simont, who later went on to become an award-winning children's book illustrator himself.

Robert McCloskey's Author–Illustrator Books (all Viking Press)

Lentil, 1940
Make Way for Ducklings, 1941 (Caldecott Medal)
Homer Price, 1943
Blueberries for Sal, 1948 (Caldecott Honor)
Centerburg Tales, 1951
One Morning in Maine, 1952 (Caldecott Honor)
Time of Wonder, 1957 (Caldecott Medal)
Burt Dow: Deep-Water Man, 1963

Books Illustrated

Yankee Doodle's Cousins. Anne Malcolmson, Houghton Mifflin, 1941.
The Man Who Lost His Head. Claire Huchet Bishop, Viking Press, 1942.
Tree Toad. Robert H. Davis, J. B. Lippincott, 1942.
Trigger John's Son. Tom Robinson, Viking Press, 1949.
Journey Cake, Ho! Ruth Sawyer, Viking Press, 1953. (Caldecott Honor)
Junket: The Dog Who Liked Everything "Just So." Anne H. White, Viking Press, 1955.
Henry Reed, Inc. Keith Robertson, Viking Press, 1958.
Henry Reed's Journey. Keith Robertson, Viking Press, 1963.
Henry Reed's Baby-Sitting Service. Keith Robertson, Viking Press, 1966.
Henry Reed's Big Show. Keith Robertson, Viking Press, 1970.

In 1945, McCloskey and his family moved to an island in Maine. This is where McCloskey drew the illustrations for most of the other books readers are familiar with, such as *Blueberries for Sal*, *One Morning in Maine*, and *Time of Wonder*. From their time on the island, his daughters Sal and Jane gained a love for the ocean and nature. They became expert clam diggers and boaters.

Important Dates in the Life and Career of Robert McCloskey

1914: Born in Hamilton, Ohio.
1932–1935: Attends art school at the Vesper George School of Art in Boston.
1935: Receives advice from editor May Massee.
1938: Shows draft of *Lentil* to May Massee.
1939: Moves to New York's Greenwich Village, where he shares a studio with illustrator Marc Simont; begins work on *Make Way for Ducklings*.
1940: *Lentil* is published; marries Margaret (Peggy) Durand, a children's librarian and the daughter of acclaimed children's book author Ruth Sawyer. (Robert and Peggy meet at a party at May Massee's New York City apartment.)
1941: *Make Way for Ducklings* is published.
1943: *Homer Price* is published.
1945: Daughter Sally is born; family moves part-time to an island in Maine.
1948: Daughter Jane is born; *Blueberries for Sal* is published; family moves to Rome for one year.
1953: *Journey Cake, Ho!*, a collaboration with mother-in-law Ruth Sawyer, is published.
1957: *Time of Wonder* is published.
1987: Nancy Schön's mallard family sculpture is installed in Boston Public Garden.
2003: Dies in Deer Isle, Maine.

Bibliography (* denotes primary source)

Film

Robert McCloskey. Film by Morton Schindel. Weston Woods, 1964. Available on Amazon Prime.

Speech

*Caldecott Medal acceptance speech. Published in *The Horn Book*, August 1942.

Books

Harrison, Barbara, and Gregory Maguire, eds. "'Bothering to Look': A Conversation Between Robert McCloskey and Ethel Heins." In *Innocence and Experience: Essays and Conversations on Children's Literature*, 326–40. New York: Lothrop, Lee & Shepard Books, 1987.

Marcus, Leonard S. *A Caldecott Celebration: Seven Artists and Their Paths to the Caldecott Medal*. New York: Walker & Co., 2008.

*Marcus, Leonard S. *Show Me a Story!: Why Picture Books Matter: Conversations with 21 of the World's Most Celebrated Illustrators*. Somerville, MA: Candlewick Press, 2012.

McCloskey, Jane. *Robert McCloskey: A Private Life in Words and Pictures*. Kittery, MI: Seapoint Books, 2011.

*Schmidt, Gary D. *Robert McCloskey*. Boston: Twayne Publishers, 1990.

William Allen White Memorial Library. *The May Massee Collection. Creative Publishing for Children, 1923–1963, a Checklist*. Emporia, Kansas: Emporia State University, 1979.

Audio Recordings

*McCloskey, Robert. "Robert McCloskey Interviewed by Anita Silvey." The Horn Book Radio Review and NPR, July 3, 1986.

"The Creative Process: A May Massee Workshop." With Robert Burch, Carolyn Field, Margaret Lesser Foster, Doris Gates, Milton Glick, and Robert McCloskey. Emporia, Kansas: Emporia State University, June 20, 1973. Unpublished.

"The May Massee Workshop on Oral History." With Robert McCloskey and Margaret McElderry. Emporia, Kansas: Emporia State University, August 1, 1983. Unpublished.

Scholarly Articles

*Heins, Ethel L. "From Mallards to Maine: A Conversation with Robert McCloskey." *Journal of Youth Services in Libraries* (Winter 1988): 187–93.

*Larrick, Nancy. "Robert McCloskey's Make Way for Ducklings." *Elementary English* 37 (March 1960): 143–48.

The original book dummy, along with a lot of other material from McCloskey (and other authors), resides at the May Massee Collection at Emporia State University.

For Everett and Cate, my own little ducklings —*EBS*
For all the aspiring illustrators out there. Go buy some ducks. —*BS*

In 1985, Boston parks officials commissioned sculptor Nancy Schön to create larger-than-life statues of the avian characters from *Make Way for Ducklings*. The statues were installed in the city's public garden, where the story concludes. Although McCloskey was initially skeptical of the project, he was immediately won over when he witnessed a child climb onto one of the ducks. Children are invited to interact with the statues and bring the story to life. Today, Bostonians regularly dress up the statues for holidays and to reflect current events.

Acknowledgments

I would like to extend my gratitude to Jane and Sally McCloskey for their warm support and help. The following people also answered questions, helped me track down photos and resources, and were generally encouraging and a source of information: Rebekah Curry at the May Massee Collection at Emporia State University; Ellen Keiter, H. Nichols Clark, and Alexandra Kennedy of the Eric Carle Museum of Picture Book Art; Meghan Melvin at the Museum of Fine Arts, Boston; and writers Gary D. Schmidt, Leonard S. Marcus, and Anita Silvey.

Picture Credits

Courtesy of Jane and Sarah McCloskey: 36, 38

Sketches for MAKE WAY FOR DUCKLINGS by Robert McCloskey, copyright 1941, renewed © 1969 by Robert McCloskey. Used by permission of Viking Children's Books, an imprint of Penguin Young Readers Group, a division of Penguin Random House LLC. All rights reserved. May Massee Collection, Emporia State University Special Collections and Archives, Emporia, Kansas: 37 (left), 39

Pen and charcoal sketch of ducklings (circa 1940) by Robert McCloskey. Resides at Boston Public Library (Drawings for Children's Books). Copyright Robert McCloskey. Courtesy of Jane and Sarah McCloskey: 39 (right)

Courtesy of Nancy Schön: 40

Calkins Creek
An imprint of Astra Books for Young Readers,
a division of Astra Publishing House
astrapublishinghouse.com
Printed in China

ISBN: 978-1-63592-392-6 (hc)
ISBN: 978-1-63592-827-3 (eBook)
Library of Congress Control Number: 2021918214

First edition
10 9 8 7 6 5 4 3 2 1

Design by Barbara Grzeslo
The text is set in Frutiger Bold Condensed.
The illustrations are created with gouache and colored pencil.